CHRIS FLAMION

Easy Cast Iron How-To's

Tips and Tricks For Cast Iron Care, Seasoning, Cooking and Cleaning

Copyright © 2023 by Chris Flamion

All rights reserved. No part of this publication may be reproduced, stored or transmitted in any form or by any means, electronic, mechanical, photocopying, recording, scanning, or otherwise without written permission from the publisher. It is illegal to copy this book, post it to a website, or distribute it by any other means without permission.

Chris Flamion asserts the moral right to be identified as the author of this work.

Chris Flamion has no responsibility for the persistence or accuracy of URLs for external or third-party Internet Websites referred to in this publication and does not guarantee that any content on such Websites is, or will remain, accurate or appropriate.

Designations used by companies to distinguish their products are often claimed as trademarks. All brand names and product names used in this book and on its cover are trade names, service marks, trademarks and registered trademarks of their respective owners. The publishers and the book are not associated with any product or vendor mentioned in this book. None of the companies referenced within the book have endorsed the book.

Second edition

This book was professionally typeset on Reedsy.
Find out more at reedsy.com

For Lydia,
The reason I do absolutely anything in this world anymore.
Thank you for keeping that fire lit under me.
Even though you don't know it.
I love you more than you can conceive.

For Amanda,
Thank you for your love and support while working on this project.
Without your help during this time this book would still be a concept.
I love you, thank you for everything.

> "This world will be yours later, I'll try to pick up a bit before I close for the night."
>
> - COREY TAYLOR (AMERICA 51)

Contents

1	Introduction	1
2	Different Types	3
3	Restoration	7
4	Cleaning	10
5	Seasoning	17
6	Cooking	22
7	**BONUS RECIPES**	26
8	Huevos Rancheros	27
9	Meaty Breakfast Casserole	29
10	Beef and Bean Stew	32
11	Irish Root Stew	34
12	Short Ribs	37
13	Cast Iron Steak	39
14	Rustic Apple Pie	41
15	Banana Upside Down Cake	43
16	βαμ Barbecue Sauce	45
17	Conclusion	47
18	Resources	49

1

Introduction

Welcome to Easy Cast Iron How-To's: Tips and Tricks for Cast Iron Care, Seasoning, Cooking, and Cleaning. My name is Christopher Flamion and I am extremely excited to be writing this book. Finally! I'll have something to give people when they keep asking me what to do with their cast iron and how to take care of it. Whether you're new to the cast iron club and just got your first piece or you're a well **seasoned** owner, I hope that this book will prove to be useful to you in some way. I have been obsessed with cast iron for many years now and if you are reading this book, you may be obsessed as well. Welcome to the club! I'm excited to share my knowledge with you that I've picked up over the years. Depending on who you are, some of the information may be controversial. But I assure you, it is all factual, whether we want to believe it or not.

If there's one thing that is found in the cast iron community it is that people are set in their ways. There's no amount of words that can go to convince a cast iron lover to change the voo-doo that they do to their iron. Properly cared for, cast iron can last for generations. In my collection I'm pretty sure that at least 2 pieces have been passed down from my Grandma to my Mom and then to me. I've cleaned rusted pieces, seasoned new ones, restored pieces for friends and even made mistakes of my own along the way to build the experiences I have. I'm hoping that this book will help you in your journey and make it so you don't have to go through the same mistakes that I did, and to just keep the enjoyment and appreciation for this magical cooking apparatus ingrained within you.

From what I remember of my obsession with cast iron, my obsession started when I was a teenager. Seeing that beautiful, shiny, heavy metal \m/ pan going from the stove top to the oven was just mind boggling. I enjoyed cooking and spent quite a bit of time in the kitchen. Typically there was always a pan for a specific job that needed done. Food could move from one pan to another, but it didn't usually travel straight from the stove top into the oven in the same pan. And later seeing that same pan going on camping trips, being put over and in the fire. Was there nothing this thing couldn't do? Breakfasts, lunches, dinners, desserts, stove top, oven, camp fires, home protection, this thing was practically indestructible and could do it all. Eventually, I would find out, yes. Indeed there are things that one should not do with the pan. The amazing thing is, aside from drilling holes or shooting it, they are actually pretty resilient. So grab your cast iron and come along as I tell you the do's and don'ts of this black beauty.

Let's get started shall we!

2

Different Types

One of the things I love about cast iron is the wide variety that is out there. I'm sure you're asking yourself, there's only two isn't there? The skillet and the big one right? Actually... no. There are many different versions of cast iron and some of them are even multi-functional. But for starters I'll make it easy and just talk about the difference between two types of cast iron before separating the styles of pans.

Bare - The type of cast iron that everyone is probably most familiar with is the bare cast iron pans. Bare cast iron pans are the ones that everyone's grandma had and they come in many different forms. Over the years they have added to the functionality and specific uses of the bare cast iron pans, I'll touch on those in a few paragraphs. Bare cast iron is the one that requires the most attention and maintenance when it comes to maintaining and keeping the longevity of the cookware.

Enameled - These types of cast iron cookware are the easiest to take care of. Enameled cast iron is produced the same way as bare. Except, when it comes time to either season or coat the pan with oil, the manufacturers coat the pan with a glass like enamel that provides that same coating and non-stick properties that are loved so much by the bare cast iron enthusiasts with proper seasoning. Enameled doesn't technically need seasoning. You can get away without doing it and your pan will do just fine. If you want the enameled cookware to last even longer and continue to look like new, there are a few things that can be done to help prevent wear and tear on it. I'll touch on that as we continue.

Skillets - I'm pretty sure we're all familiar with skillets. They are the pans with long handles typically used on the stovetop. Skillets are useful for all kinds of cooking - steaks, eggs, and sauteing. Most things can be cooked in skillets and they'll turn out just fine. These are even used with desserts. The great part about cast iron is that they can go from the stove to the oven and finish there. If you are a person who understands that you can make a great steak in the oven, sear it in a hot skillet and then transfer it to a hot oven to slowly finish cooking, it is amazing!

The skillet comes in many shapes and sizes. From very large ones that could hold numerous steaks to really small ones, these things are versatile. I have a small one that I have used primarily for eggs. But I know many restaurants will use small cast iron skillets for desserts such as a big cookie, lava cake, or bread pudding.

Dutch Ovens - Dutch ovens can be better thought of as pots. They are deeper cookware that is also used primarily for soups and stews, but also can be used for most things that would require a lid. Even if it doesn't need a lid per se, the dutch oven is better thought of as all around cookware for when you go camping. It can do everything a skillet can do, you can still saute and cook normal food in it. But if you need to make bread or bake some beans or make a stew while out in the woods, the dutch oven should be your go to. The sizes of dutch ovens can vary just as much as the skillets, I've seen them range from large ones to create many stews or roast whole chickens in, to as small as what is used for a bowl of soup.

The dutch oven will come with a lid. There are different schools of thought as to the purpose of the lid. Well, it's just to cover the food, duh. Not exactly. There are different types of lids for different purposes. One of the great things about dutch ovens and why it has the name oven in it, is that it can be used as such. With the lid on, you can fully cover it in coals and instead of just having heat from the bottom where the fire is, the heat can radiate from all around this piece. Some lids are designed with little spikes or bumps on the bottom portion of the lid. These bumps are very beneficial when it comes to cooking chickens or roasts. While the food cooks steam builds up, condenses, and liquid builds on the lid. Instead of that liquid running down the side it actually drips from the lid and bastes the food while it cooks without having to open the lid to do it yourself. Pretty ingenious if you ask me.

Griddles/Flattops - Big flat piece of metal? Yes please! Griddles have really made a boom lately in the home grilling market. People were once worried about grill marks and now they just want that extra cooking space. Griddles are great for family cooking, lots of food on a flat surface. Typically griddles are found on home use grills or in restaurants. However, there are some stove tops, gas and even electric models that are used for griddles and can span multiple burners to provide the space.

There are many different sizes of griddles available too. With more space comes more that you're able to cook at once. Especially if it's in the form of a grill, that can really go a long way when camping. Sure, you won't be making a soup unless you use another pot or dutch oven on top of it. Just about everything else can be made. Steaks? Absolutely, and instead of only fitting one or two in a pan, how about six, or even ten steaks?

Others - This is to cover many of the other odds and ends that are out there. If it can be cooked with, I'm sure there's a cast iron version of it. There are presses for sandwiches and paninis. There are different baking style pans that are used for cornbread, brownies, breads, cakes and pizzas. Also, there are specialty shaped ones too to get a fancy or desired shape with certain foods too. The cookware that is made with cast iron is seemingly endless. Every time I feel like I've found them all, something else comes up. Whether it's just a different shape or design. It's something new.

One thing to keep in mind with a lot of these odds and ends pieces is that most of them are manufactured in the bare style of pan. Where that's not really a problem, and will typically come preseasoned, it is something to keep in mind when you're looking to expand your collection. With those pieces you would just follow the same routine for seasoning that will be addressed later in this book.

3

Restoration

There are many reasons why you may need to restore a cast iron pan back to its original glory. Whether you have been given a piece from a family member or friend that doesn't know what to do with it or just doesn't want it. Or maybe you found it at a garage sale and clearly the people you got it from didn't take the time to take care of it. The good news is, once you get this black beauty back to her original glory and keep up with the maintenance, it'll last for years to come. Even you will be able to pass it on to future generations. I'm just happy that you're deciding to do it.

I've seen some pans that were completely destroyed and one would think that there is no coming back from that. That's the great thing about cast iron. Aside from holes or really deep corrosion these pieces can be pulled back from the dead. I've seen pieces that were forgotten about while camping and left partially in the dirt. During that time, water had its way with the metal and started eating away at some of the metal and rusted the rest of it. The worst one that I personally restored was left submerged in water and fully rusted. During this section you will do things to your cookware that I would not suggest you do at any other time other than doing a full restoration like we're about to do. There are a few pieces of equipment that you will need and depending on your budget and availability of these items, you may be putting in more effort than someone else with different items.

First and foremost, safety first, so I strongly suggest you wear a dust mask during this process. Also, depending on which piece of equipment you will be using, wear safety glasses. Some of the things you will be needing during this section if you have them are: dust masks, safety glasses, right angle sander, sand paper (various grits), angle grinder, water, soap, abrasive scrubbing pad.

The first step in this process is to see exactly how bad the damage is that we're working with. I suggest giving the pan just a quick wash with soapy water to knock off big chunks of dirt or build up and see how bad things are. Do not be afraid to take off the seasoning during this part, if there's any left, we will be building that back up and starting from scratch. Once you've cleaned away the big stuff and have assessed the damage, if it's not too bad, you can move on to the "cleaning" or "seasoning" sections of this book. If there's still a lot of work to do, we're about to get dirty.

If there are large divots or corrosion spots in or around the pan, that is where the angle grinder is going to come into play. Use the angle grinder to smooth out the big holes that have eaten into the metal or even just to smooth out the rest of the pan quicker. If you don't have access to an angle grinder, I'd suggest trying to find one and borrow it. Otherwise, you're going to be spending a lot of time sanding. You'll want to start with a sand paper with a grit with a lower number. The lower the grit of the sandpaper, the rougher and more gouging power the sandpaper has. You want to do this over the entire pan until the rough spots have become smoother, not necessarily smooth, but smoother.

From here, it's a matter of preference. I've seen people increase the sandpaper grit into the hundreds, until they get an ultra smooth finish on the pan. I'd say, it depends on how far you want to take it down. You really wouldn't have to go any farther than 180 - 200 grit. Sanding down the metal that far would be more than enough to make it smooth and strip the pan down to the base metal and get it ready for reseasoning. There will probably still be slight dips and divots that you may see in the metal. These will more than likely be from the casting process. These beauty marks will be fine and once you season the pan again, this will be mirror smooth and you'll be so happy that you've gone through this process to restore the pan.

At this point you should be looking at a shiny naked piece of metal. After grinding, sanding, and making sure that all of the rust and corrosion is removed from the pan, we're ready to start the process of making this the best and longest lasting pan you've ever owned. After you've done all of the above steps, go ahead one more time and clean it off with soap and water. Make sure to dry it thoroughly so no new rust or anything starts while we get ready to season it. One thing I would suggest to get it ready for seasoning after cleaning is to put the pan in a 450F - 500F oven for 30 minutes. Once the time is up, turn off the oven and let the oven and pan cool naturally. This will get the pan ready for the next steps. Or you could make sure that all of the previous oils are removed from the pan before continuing. If your oven has a self cleaning cycle, put the pan in for the whole cycle. That will get rid of everything and should strip the pan down to its bare metal.

4

Cleaning

Fact or Fiction: You can clean your cast iron with hot soapy water? True

First thing I'll address in this section is the soap issue. I know there are people out there, younger me included, that will argue tooth and nail that you never NEVER use soap on your cast iron, don't do it. Well... here's the thing, it's not going to hurt it. It's really not. What does soap do? It loosens grease, food, dirt, oil, and washes it away. If a cast iron pan is properly seasoned, which we'll address in the next section, then there's really nothing to worry about. You won't wash away a good seasoning with some soap and water. If you're worried about washing away your seasoning from your pan with soap and water, stop using your pan as a bacon grease holder and season the pan right.

Sorry, I had to deal with that real quick. Now that the soap issue has been dealt with, let's get started with the cleaning of the bare cast iron pan. Depending on how bad the pan is will depend on exactly how you will approach this. For most messes, be it cooked on stuck food, rust, or whatever, you can get away with using salt, a dish rag, and some good ol' fashioned elbow grease. They do make certain scrubbing pads, or even pieces of chainmail that can be used for this part. I'm not against them, but they are not the ways I'll be touching on here. They can be used, and you would just use them like you would any other scrubbing device. Don't put too much pressure because you don't want to scrape through the seasoning to bare metal with them, especially the chainmail.

Bare

- With this option you will be going through a good amount of salt. Depending on the size of the pan, I'd say put half a cup to a full cup of salt into the pan and use the rag to scrub. You can use a paper towel, but from my experience, the tiny salt rocks while scrubbing all the junk off of the pan, will also shred the paper towel and it's better to just not deal with tiny pieces of paper at the same time. If you're trying to scrub away food or something that is really caked on the pan, you can add a small amount of water to the salt to make it like a paste and put it on the stove to heat up. The water, heat, and salt, has yet to be unable to remove any issues I've had.

You may need to refresh the salt after a while of scrubbing this way. You may notice, as you are scrubbing, the salt will go from bigger chunks of white salt to more of a powder. Depending on what you are trying to remove from the pan, the salt will change colors as well. So as you scrub, change the salt as many times as you need. Once it is salt dust, and seems to be no longer breaking down what is in the pan, switch it out. Like I said at the beginning of this section, it is likely that you will be going through a lot of salt. It's ok, this is normal.

EASY CAST IRON HOW-TO'S

1. Once you have scrubbed the ever loving hell out of the pan it's time for the soapy water. *insert scary organ music* This will finish breaking down any bits of food that may have made it past the salt, help to remove the salt, and break down any of the old oil that has not stuck to the pan in the past. This makes it so that with your next seasoning, it will have a better polymerization and less likely to chip off or be sticky. Since you did all the scrubbing with the salt in the first step, you really don't have to go at this with a brillo pad or anything. Just some warm to hot soapy water and the soft side of a sponge will do the trick. We're not scraping this thing down to bare metal here, just cleaning it. Another thing to keep in mind is that yes, while using the cast iron over time, there will be slight layers building up over time that will also alter the flavor, if even just slightly. I'm a fan of using soap to get rid of any possible residual flavors because I don't want my apple pie or peach cobbler to taste like fish. I'm not a fan of that. Just use the soap and season your pan correctly.

2. Dry this thing off! This is one of the more important steps for taking care of cast iron pans. Dry all of it, everything you can get to. The inside, outside, handle, all of it. This thing is made out of iron. If you leave this to sit with water in it or improperly dry it, it will rust. Then you'll be in the same boat as before, having to scrub all the rust out and starting this process all over again. Believe me, it can be super frustrating having to do that. Iron rusts surprisingly fast too. Even a little bit is not ok, so make sure that when you're done washing it you dry it thoroughly. I will usually dry it out with a dish towel and then put it on the stove top for a few minutes just to make sure that all the water has evaporated off of the pan.

3. At this point you can take a little bit of oil with a paper towel or a rag to coat the cooking surface of the pan. If you heated up the pan to finish drying it out, this works out perfectly for this because the oil that you are adding to it now, you want to be added to the other layers of seasoning and get cooked on a little bit. After adding the oil, just let the pan cool and then store it wherever you choose. Some people decide to keep the cast iron in the oven, some keep it in the storage underneath the oven. I personally have a rack that I keep my cast iron on. The racks are spaced such that I am able to keep a dutch oven at the bottom, and about 5 or so skillets getting smaller as it gets higher. I like this option because it keeps all of my cast iron pans right there on my counter stacked neatly and ready to use.

I have one really important thing I want to say at the end of this and it's important to keep in mind when you are storing your cast iron. Make sure that you use a towel or rag and wipe away any and all excess oil left on the pan. If you store your pan with extra oil, that oil will become sticky over time. It feels disgusting when you go to pick up a pan that you're excited to use and should be clean, but no matter where you touch it your hand sticks like the last person to use it was a toddler who came back from a cotton candy party. You won't like this, trust me… it's NOT cotton candy. This is more common with large pieces. You'll think you need more oil than you actually do and instead of just using extra paper towels and getting rid of it, you just put it away covered. You don't want this in your life. Just wipe off the excess and you'll be fine.

Enameled

EASY CAST IRON HOW-TO'S

1. Enameled is very easy to clean. This is probably the biggest perk to using enameled over the bare metal pans. These pans already have a coating that isn't really coming off unless you go at it with some hard metal and really try and scrape it off. You are able to just use some hot soapy water and scrub off what you need to. Depending on how stuck on some foods may be, you may want to add the soapy water and place on a burner like with the bare metal version of cleaning. What this does is, it increases the temperature of the water, pan, and food, and actually causes the food to absorb some of the water which loosens the grip that the food has on the pan and makes it easier to scrape off. If you feel like you really need to scrub at the food to get it off, I would suggest something soft that isn't going to gouge the enamel on the pan, like a wooden spoon or spatula. Wooden utensils are great for this kind of thing.

2. Once you have scraped and cleaned the pan with soapy water and rinsed it off, dry it off. This part isn't as direly important as with bare cast iron pans, but you still don't want to just let the pan sit around with water in it just in case. If there is a little crack or scratch in the enamel and the water does happen to get through, you will start to rust your pan and not even realize it. And that doesn't taste good, not to mention isn't healthy to eat either.

3. This step is kind of two steps put together. There are different types of enameled pans and some of them have a ring around the top separating the inside and outside of the pan that is bare. If yours has this, I typically will dab just a tiny bit of oil on a piece of paper towel and coat that ring. This isn't as crucial as it is in the bare metal cast iron pans, but you still want to try and stop your pan from rusting any way you possibly can. If your enameled pan doesn't have that ring, then just dry it off and store it. You

can store it in the oven, the pantry, the drawer beneath the oven, a rack for pans, or wherever you see fit. My mom keeps out a small cast iron pan that she uses pretty close to every day to cook their breakfast and that thing never leaves the stove top. So if your plan is to use it tomorrow or soon enough that you don't see the need for putting it away, then don't. I think the look of a stove with a cast iron pan sitting on it looks like you mean business anyways, even if you don't use it.

Storage

Ok, I just wanted to touch on this part one more time. I did mention it in the processes mentioned above but there's just a couple of things I wanted to touch on again.

First, never, and I mean NEVER, put your cast iron away wet. This will lead to the iron rusting and ruining all of the hard work you have done to season and take care of your pan. Sometimes, you don't even really think about it. I've done it numerous times. You start to clean it, something is really stubborn and you think I'll get to this in a little bit. Even waiting an hour, that water can start to work on that iron and it can start ruining things that quickly. I've learned it's just easier to clean it once you finish using it. This is one of those pans you don't want to "let soak." Yeah, I'm looking at you, you know who you are.

Second, if you're going to stack your cast iron, I would suggest it only be your enameled cast iron. However, if you are going to stack your bare cast iron, I would try and keep it to only two pieces you stack on one another. The issue with stacking is that the weight can cause the top pan to scratch and dig into the coating of the bottom pan which again, will just put us in a bad situation and leave the pan open to rust and other issues down the line. Also with stacking them, this will multiply the chances of liquid build up and rust with the pans. Instead of getting rust on only one pan, now you've got rust on two and have to fix and reseason both pans. Usually this happens when you don't properly dry the bottom of the pan you put on the inside of the other. The water sits there and then they both rust. Not good.

The final thing to keep in mind also goes hand in hand with proper seasoning. As I mentioned with the bare pan storage, be sure to wipe away as much excess oil as you can. Similar to how water multiplies when you have the pans stacked on one another, so does the oil. You might not think that wiping away the oil from the bottom is important, but once it is inside the other pan, now that bottom pan has excess oil and as it sits and builds up, it has the possibility to get sticky and, separate and attract water which, you guessed it, can lead to rust. Typically after seasoning, when you add a tiny amount of oil to the inside cooking surface of the pan, I don't worry about adding the oil to the outside. It's important to be seasoned, but the added bit is redundant and not needed to the outside at that point.

5

Seasoning

Fact or Fiction: Bacon and lard are the best things to season a cast iron pan with? FALSE

There are many things that make cast iron amazing to work with, but probably the most important part, the thing that will make or break a person's love with cast iron, is the seasoning. Put simply, the seasoning for a cast iron pan is what makes the pan non-stick. Most pans nowadays come pre seasoned which is helpful, but it's a good habit to season your own and coat the pan regularly with use. Without this seasoning, it will be virtually impossible to be able to cook anything in your pan and have it release and be able to be moved around in the pan. Ever have eggs stick to a pan? In a copper or Teflon pan, that can be messy enough, but in a cast iron pan, when you have all of the grooves and ridges to contend with, when something like that gets stuck, it can become a nightmare to clean.

What seasoning is, is a layer, or build up of layers, of fatty oils that get cooked into the pan and form a hard coating on the surface of the pan and fill in the grooves. This process is called polymerization. When you season a pan, you want to season the entire thing. The inside and the outside. There is a lot to consider when you do this too - different oils, flavors, smoke points, amounts, and temperatures. I will touch on all of those in the next few pages to hopefully help ease your stress of what to do when it comes to seasoning your cast iron. I hope that you have followed the other parts of this book for cleaning to make sure that your pan is now ready for the seasoning process. We want the pan to be clean because if we try to season a cast iron pan while there are bits of food or carbon build up on the pan, the seasoning will not fully adhere and will easily chip away in those spots and start to spread throughout the pan. If you're going to do it, might as well do it right.

One of the first things to consider is the oil that you are going to want to use for the seasoning. Some people think that fat is fat, so any kind of fat will do for seasoning cast iron. This isn't true. I'll start by trying to get back the people who I lost, reading the fact or fiction above. First, the average user of cast iron will use their pan a handful of times a year. Even if a person uses their pan once a month, that is getting really close to the line on a pan I would consider being ok for bacon grease or lard. I'm not saying it can't be used, it's just not the best option. If you don't use your pan often enough, that bacon grease or lard that you used on your pan can and will go rancid. For me, I'd rather not risk it and have to deal with the cleaning and going through all of the steps again. I would prefer to have a well seasoned pan that I can cook bacon in and just season it for better long term storage, just in case it happens to sit a while.

Some of the other things to consider when seasoning your pan is what the smoke point of the oil you're using is. One thing I see happen, and I've done it myself when I was starting out, is while seasoning, not bringing the oil to the smoke point. When the smoke point is not reached, you are not properly bonding the oil to the pan. Typically this

SEASONING

is when the pan will come out sticky and not smooth like it should be. Smoke point is important when seasoning your pan. You wouldn't want to use an oil that has a smoke point of 450° in an oven that is set to 350° to season it, that just won't work. In the table below I will lay out some options and their smoke points. Then, we'll get to the seasoning.

Flaxseed Oil	225°F
Bacon Grease	325°F
Lard	375°F
Olive Oil	375°F
Canola Oil	400°F
Vegetable Oil	400°F - 450°F
Sunflower Oil	400°F - 450°F
Grapeseed Oil	420°F
Peanut Oil	450°F
Coconut Oil	450°F
Avocado	520°F

Before I get to the seasoning process, I just want to say a few words to consider with the above oils. I've already discussed bacon and lard, so I'll leave them alone here. Typically, the way these numbers will read, the lower the smoke point, the easier the oil will be on your wallet. The higher the smoke point, the more expensive it is. Also, the lower smoke point oils have a tendency to create a more brittle and flakey seasoning. Aside from coconut oil, I never really noticed any discerning tastes from the oils while cooking with the pan later. But if you are sensitive to any of the above tastes, then you may prefer something else to use. And the last bit of advice I want to give is to know who you are cooking for or who may be in contact with the pan or the stuff you are cooking with. Although it's not likely that using peanut oil will cause an allergic reaction to someone allergic to peanuts. Some peanut oils that aren't highly refined could. Best bet, and best safe practice, if someones allergic, don't risk it.

Get on with it already! How do we season this thing?!

Ok. Let's do this.

1. Determine which oil you want to use and preheat your oven accordingly. I typically add about 50 degrees to the smoke point and that is where I set my oven. So if you're using an oil with a smoke point of 400F, I'll set my oven to 450F.
2. Apply a tiny amount of oil to the pan. About a teaspoon
3. Use a paper towel or rag to spread the oil all around the pan. Cooking surface, outside, handle, bottom, all of it.
4. After spreading the oil all around the pan, use a fresh paper towel or spot of the towel and wipe up all excess oil. I will normally let the pan sit for a few minutes first, just to let the oil settle.
5. Place the pan in your preheated oven on the center rack. Place a sheet of aluminum to catch any excess oil that may drip off. If you did the above step correctly, this shouldn't be an issue. But, just to be sure.
6. Bake your cast iron for about 45 - 60 minutes. **THERE WILL BE SOME SMOKE.**
7. At this point, your pan has been seasoned and you have a few options. If you desire to put more layers on the pan, repeat steps

2-6.

8. The pan may be good to go at this point, in which case, all you have to do is turn off the oven and let the pan cool naturally.
9. When all is said and done, apply a TINY amount of oil to the cooking surface of the pan and rub it in completely and wipe away the excess.

Congratulations! You seasoned your cast iron pan! See, that wasn't so scary. People often wonder how often they have to season their cast iron. Now that you have seasoned your pan, all it takes now to maintain is proper care which I went over in previous sections of this book. From this point forward it should only take little bits of oil after cooking to keep this black beauty pristine. If a dish isn't terribly messy, like frying eggs or something that hasn't left a lot of junk in the pan, there's nothing wrong with wiping it out. If there was oil involved, that oil can count as the oil that would normally be added at the end for storage.

The easiest and most effective way to keep your pan seasoned and in amazing shape is to use it. That's right, if you just use the pan, over time the more you cook and keep adding different oils to the layers, the seasoning will build up and it will become stronger and more effective. I know it's nice to have a rustic piece to bust out from time to time and show off, but really, the best way to take care of these is to use them regularly and just show them the proper care they deserve. Do these things and you will own a piece of cookware that you'll be able to pass down through your family as well.

6

Cooking

Cooking with cast iron is incredibly beneficial. The amount of heat that these pans can withstand and hold onto is great in the kitchen. A good hot pan can be great for searing, sauteing, heating frying oil, or just for keeping something warm. The heat that is stored in the cast iron will last long after you've removed it from the heat as well. One thing that most people don't know is that cast iron is actually induction cooktop ready. Yeah, you heard me… well… read me. Induction cooktops are not the topic of this book, but they are pretty amazing. Check them out if you haven't, but they work by heating pans with magnets. And cast iron, as old of a pan as it is, is perfect for induction cooking. One thing you'll have to worry about is possibly the weight, as with everything else with cast iron. This stuff can really add up.

When cooking with cast iron, the part that everyone dreads is probably the whole reason you're all here, the sticking. Food sticking to cast iron is a pretty common issue with new cast iron users and some old timers too. But, knowing how to combat the sticking and understanding why it sticks goes a long way in helping to make sure it doesn't happen. First off, other than the layer of seasoning which is going to be your best friend when it comes to cooking with cast iron, you want to make sure that you have plenty of oil or "fats" in the pan while you're cooking. The things that tend to really stick the most when cooking in cast iron pans are things high in protein. So when you're doing those - eggs, steaks, chicken, what have you, make sure that you also add a bit of extra insurance and put some extra fat in the pan.

A lot of times when sticking happens, it's usually when you add the protein to the pan right after cooking something else. So a lot of the oils have already been used to coat the first thing you've started cooking, then you add eggs or something like that to the pan and there's not enough oil to help fully create that barrier to help keep them from sticking to the pan. Make sure there is enough fat in the pan to be able to take in the ingredient. If sticking does occur, one way to try and help things loosen up is to turn down the heat and cover the pan. This traps in the moisture and will slowly start to soften the grip that the food has on the pan and you should be able to scrape it loose after that. Other foods that happen to stick are meats like steaks and chicken. This one is kind of hard to read. Usually when it comes to those, if you're sure that there is enough fat in the pan, just let it go and don't touch it, just leave it alone. Meat will initially stick to almost any pan you put it in and once it has a sear it will naturally release itself from the pan. This is normal and also lends itself to great flavor. A steak with a good seared outside tastes so much better than one without. Just let it cook and release itself.

Like in the cleaning portion of this book, I had to push against the belief that you should never use soap while cleaning a cast iron pan. With cooking, there are some Other beliefs as well. The biggest one being that you shouldn't cook with tomatoes or tomato sauce because of the acidity of them. The thought is that the increased acidity of the tomatoes will eat away at the pan or leach into the pan and give things a metallic taste. This is not the case in my experience. A well seasoned pan has absolutely no problem cooking tomatoes or other things with high acidity.

I prefer cooking with wooden utensils, I always have, that's just my preference. Be it on cast iron, copper pans, non-stick Teflon pans, whatever. Wooden is my preference. But, I feel like it's also another important thing to not have you worry about metal utensils when it comes to cooking with cast iron. Metal utensils are completely safe and can be used when cooking with cast iron. I feel like it goes without saying that you shouldn't be gouging at the pan with them. But, using the utensils for their intended purpose, is completely fine. Plus, with the reapplying of a layer of oil after and usually before you start cooking anyways. You'll be perfectly fine even if you do get carried away a little bit and scratch into the seasoning some.

When cooking with cast iron indoors, other than the weight, there's not too much to worry about. These pans are able to handle high heat and can cook most anything in them. Where they really show their versatility is being able to go from the stovetop to the oven. So while your oven is preheating, you could be getting everything sauteed or seared in the pan on the stovetop and then, when it's time for you to throw in the steak, casserole, pie, or cake, you just take it from the burner and put it right into the oven. You don't need to worry about ruining the pan cooking like this. You'll ruin your food before you do anything to the pan. And this part should be pretty common thinking, but, since the pan does such a great job at retaining and dissipating heat throughout the whole pan, make sure that whenever you are handling it, you use a rag, towel, handle grip or something to stop you from burning yourself.

The way most people probably remember seeing cast iron being used is in outdoor cooking. Going into the woods, camping, or using an RV or anything like that, most people have at least one skillet or one dutch oven that is their go to. In my opinion, outdoor cooking is where cast iron shines. It's so heavy duty and able to withstand heat, that depending what you're trying to cook, you are able to literally bury dutch ovens in coals and fire to cook what's inside and not worry about causing damage to the cookware. If a campfire is being used for the cooking, a dutch oven will more than likely be your best bet. I would also suggest building or bringing some sort of tripod or something to hang the dutch oven from over the fire. This is just to keep it out of the fire for you to be able to do what you have to do without fighting the fire for it.

Another good place for cast iron to be used is on a grill. Especially since there are high amounts of heat that are generated on the grill, cast iron does a great job of spreading that heat out across a wider area and being able to regulate the heat a bit better than having a 2" spot of pan that's 900F. Moving the pan around a little while cooking too can help spread that heat around and make it a lot easier to use and cook things more evenly. Whether you're cooking with charcoal or propane, I'm not getting into that debate here, cast iron is an amazing thing to use. I myself have a grill that is half charcoal grill, half propane griddle and all beautiful cast iron. I'll still use a cast iron skillet between both of them. No other cookware has the versatility that cast iron does. Just be sure whenever you're using them, that they are well seasoned and that you properly clean them after. You want more than just one good use out of your pan.

7

BONUS RECIPES

8

Huevos Rancheros

Equipment:
Cast Iron Skillet

Ingredients:

- 3 tbsp cooking oil
- 4 6" corn tortilla
- 8oz sausage(Spicy preferred)
- 1 cup refried beans
- 1 cup black beans
- 3 (4.5)oz cans green chilies
- ½ cup onion
- 3 large tomatoes
- ½ tsp salt
- 2 tsp cornstarch
- 1 tbsp water
- 4 large eggs
- 4oz Shredded Cheese
- 1 clove garlic

Instructions:

1. Drain excess liquid from chillies, chop the onion and tomatoes, and mince the garlic.
2. Heat 2 tbsp oil in a skillet. Cook tortillas slightly about 10 sec/side set on a paper towel to drain.
3. Brown the sausage and drain the fat.
4. Heat 1 tbsp of oil in a skillet. Cook onion and garlic until tender.
5. Mix sausage, beans and 2 cans of chilies.
6. Stir in tomatoes, remaining chilies and salt. Bring to a boil.
7. Cook until tomatoes are tender. Then mix in water and cornstarch.
8. While simmering, crack open eggs and top mixture.
9. Cook eggs until desired doneness while continuing to mix mixture around eggs so it doesn't stick.

There are a few different ways that you can finish this dish. Serving the food on plates with the tortillas underneath is a popular way of serving it. Some people will keep them separate and use the tortilla to scoop, pinch, or wrap the mixture and eat it that way. From there the cheese can be melted on the entire dish, on individual servings, after it's all on the tortilla, however you see fit. It's food! Have fun and enjoy this delicious meal!

9

Meaty Breakfast Casserole

Meaty Breakfast Casserole
Equipment:
Cast Iron Dutch Oven

Ingredients:

- 1 lb bacon
- 1 lb ground breakfast sausage
- 1 red bell pepper, diced
- 1 hot pepper(serrano preferred)diced
- 1 large white onion, diced
- 2 lbs frozen hash browns
- 1 cup shredded pepper jack cheese
- 1 cup shredded cheddar cheese
- 10 eggs
- smoked paprika
- salt and pepper

Instructions:

1. Preheat oven to 350F
2. Cut bacon into chunks and add to dutch oven over medium-high heat. Cook until browned and to desired doneness. Move cooked bacon to paper towel, Drain excess grease leaving about 2 tbsp in the pan.
3. Add sausage to dutch oven and brown, stirring occasionally. Stir in onion, and peppers.
4. After cooking onions and peppers for a few minutes, before they're fully cooked, add hashbrowns and stir in sausage mixture. Continue to cook until onions and peppers are tender. Add Salt, pepper, and smoked paprika to taste.
5. Whisk 6 eggs and pour over sausage mixture. Top with bacon and put in the oven for 40-45 minutes.
6. Add both cheeses to the top of the casserole and put back in the oven until the cheese melts, about 5-10 minutes.
7. Once cheese is good and melted, top the casserole with the remaining eggs, and let them cook sunny side up style. About another 5-10 minutes, just keep an eye on them.

This makes a delicious hearty breakfast casserole meal that is amazing when out in the woods. It's filling and full of flavor. You can obviously top this with whatever cheese you desire, but just know that if you add more cheese to it you will have to account for that with the cooking time. When it comes to the eggs on top. You can just crack them and leave them on top, or the way I've done it sometimes is that I would mix the eggs only slightly before putting them on top. That way they're not fully mixed yellow like scrambled eggs, and there's swirls of egg whites and yolks.To me, seasoning heavily with pepper is the way to go with

MEATY BREAKFAST CASSEROLE

this dish. It feels so rustic and tastes so good!

10

Beef and Bean Stew

Equipment:
Cast Iron Dutch Oven

Ingredients:

- 1 lb lean steak or roast, cut into cubes
- 1 tbsp vegetable oil
- 28 oz tomato juice
- 2(15oz) cans red beans, not drained
- ½ cup cooking sherry or wine
- 1 tsp sugar
- ½ tsp basil
- 1 tsp garlic powder
- ½ tsp thyme leaves
- ⅛ tsp black pepper
- 1 tsp salt
- 4 large potatoes, cubed
- 3 white onions, cut into wedges
- 4 large carrots, cut into ½" chunks

BEEF AND BEAN STEW

Instructions:

1. Put oil in dutch oven and brown the meat.
2. Add tomato juice, beans, sherry, sugar, basil, garlic, thyme, pepper, and salt. Simmer for 1 hour or until the meat is tender.
3. Add potatoes, onions and carrots. Continue to simmer for an additional 30 minutes.
4. The longer you cook this stew, the more the flavors will blend with each other, and make the potatoes and carrots more tender.

This hearty stew is great on those afternoons when you want to just sit outside, relax and just take in the view. This is a good mix of light tasting and meaty. It's delicious. Make this and sit out with the family in the fall and enjoy the flavors and feelings of the food and the weather all mixed together. It's a great feeling. It's an experience all on its own. A good moment to just sit back, relax, turn off the phone, and just enjoy life and family. Give it a shot. You won't be sorry.

11

Irish Root Stew

Equipment:

Cast Iron Dutch Oven

Ingredients:

- 1 tbsp Butter or Oil
- 1 Large Yellow Onion
- 2 Leeks, white and pale green parts only
- 4 Cloves Garlic, Diced
- 1 Stalk Celery, cut into chunks
- 5 large Potatoes, Cubed
- 5 cups Vegetable Stock
- 1 ½ cups Carrots, Sliced
- 3 tbsp Chopped Green Onion
- ⅔ cup heavy cream
- Salt and Pepper
- Shredded Cheddar Cheese(Optional)

IRISH ROOT STEW

Instructions:

1. Heat butter or oil in a cast iron pot over medium heat. Add onion, leeks, garlic, and celery and cook until tender.
2. Add 4 cups of vegetable stock to the pot. Add potatoes and bring to a boil. Reduce the heat to medium low and simmer for about 20 minutes.
3. Divide the stew into 3 parts. Allowing it to cool a bit.
4. After the stew has cooled some and is safe to blend, add 1 part to a blender and blend until creamy and smooth. Repeat the process with a second part of cooled stew.
5. Cook the carrots in the remaining 1 cup of vegetable stock, about 5 minutes.
6. Once carrots are tender add the blended puree back to the dutch oven.
7. Add Green onion and heavy cream, stirring and cooking for an additional 5 minutes.
8. Salt and pepper to taste and top with cheddar cheese.

I have made this stew many many times! It is definitely a favorite of mine. There are many different variations you can make of it too. I've made it for vegans, by swapping out cream, butter, and cheese for alternatives. Meat eaters too can have a little extra and add some bacon bits as a nice touch. It tastes like a loaded mashed potato in soup form. It's especially great during the winter months. It's a delicious hearty stew. Depending on how chunky you want it, you can blend more or less of it during that step. I've blended as much as all of it, and as little as half of a single part. ⅔ of it is the sweet spot for me, the potatoes break down nicely and thicken it up and keeping that last ⅓ is good for the chunks. Give this a try! You'll have a new favorite for those winter nights to warm your soul!

12

Short Ribs

Equipment:
Cast Iron Dutch Oven

Ingredients:

- 6 lbs short ribs cut into single ribs
- 4 carrots, cut into chunks
- 1 onion, cut into chunks
- 4 cloves garlic, diced
- 1 tbsp oil
- 3 tbsp BBQ dry rub seasoning
- 16 oz tomato sauce
- 1 cup beef broth
- ¼ cup brown sugar

Instructions:

1. Coat short ribs in BBQ dry rub. Use as much or as little as you

would prefer. I typically coat 2 sides thoroughly and lightly on the others.
2. Heat oil on high heat in dutch oven.
3. Add short ribs to the dutch oven and sear all sides.
4. Once ribs are all seared, remove from dutch oven and set aside.
5. Add carrots, onions, and garlic to dutch oven. Cook for 3-5 minutes.
6. Add tomato sauce, beef broth, and brown sugar to the pan and mix.
7. Put short ribs back in dutch oven, cover and simmer for 3-4 hours.
8. Ribs are ready when you're easily able to pull the bones from the meat.

This makes some deliciously tender short ribs! It all comes down to the type of ingredients you use too. Like all cooking, once you find out what a recipe tastes like you start to switch it up a little and experiment with different things. For this one I prefer the flavor of dark brown sugar. Plus, if you're not using Better Than Bouillon, I don't know what you're doing with your life. I fell in love with that brand years ago and other than when I make broths and stocks myself, that's what I prefer. I said 3 tbsp as an approximate amount, really it's up to you, you can go with none, or coat every side of the ribs and add extra to the pot. It's all up to you. Make it to your preferred taste. That's the great thing about cooking. Take all of these recipes as base ideas and really have fun with it, enjoy your food!

13

Cast Iron Steak

Equipment:

Cast Iron Skillet

Ingredients:

- 1 steak (T-bone, chuck, ribeye, etc.)
- 1 large onion, julienned (thinly sliced)
- 8 oz mushrooms, cleaned and sliced
- 5 cloves garlic, peeled
- 2 tbsp dry steak seasoning (optional)
- salt
- pepper
- 2 tbsp grapeseed oil
- 2 tbsp butter

Instructions:

1. Set the steak out to warm to room temperature approximately

10-20 minutes before cooking.
2. Heavily season both sides and edges of the steak with the salt and pepper. If you prefer steak seasoning, use that.
3. Place the skillet over high heat and add oil.
4. Once the skillet is beginning to lightly smoke, place steak in the pan and press all around making sure there is good contact throughout the steak.
5. DO NOT TOUCH THE STEAK!!! For 3-5 minutes
6. Flip the steak and do not move the steak again until it's finished.
7. During this time, add the butter to the pan along with the garlic cloves.
8. Cook the steak for another 3-5 minutes basting with the garlic oil and butter mixture about every 30 seconds.
9. Once the steak is to your preferred doneness remove the steak and garlic and let it sit for 5 minutes.
10. Saute onions and mushrooms in the oil and butter until they're tender. Use these to top steaks.

This is the best way to make a steak in the skillet. The reason I say to use the grapeseed oil is because it has a neutral flavor as well as a high smoke point which we want to use to create a great sear on the steak. It all depends on your preference as to whether you want to use steak seasoning or just salt and pepper. The mushrooms and onions are a great way to top the steak too. And you definitely want to let the steak rest. Resting the steak will make it stay juicy and keep all of that added flavor locked in and on the steak. Trust me, your patience will be rewarded.

14

Rustic Apple Pie

Equipment:
Cast Iron Skillet

Ingredients:

- 2 lbs Granny Smith apples
- 2 lbs Pink Lady apples
- 1 tsp ground cinnamon *or more if desired
- ¾ cup sugar
- ½ cup butter
- 1 cup brown sugar(I prefer dark)
- 2 pie crusts
- 1 egg white
- 2 tbsp sugar

Instructions:

1. Preheat the oven to 350°F.
2. In a skillet, melt butter over medium heat and add brown sugar. Cook until dissolved, stirring continuously. Once dissolved, remove from heat and let cool.
3. Peel apples and cut into wedges, approximately ½" thick. Toss apples with cinnamon and white sugar.
4. In the skillet with the brown sugar, place 1 pie crust to cover the bottom. If the pie crust is big enough, bring the crust up the edges of the skillet.
5. Dump the apple mixture into the skillet on top of the pie crust. Cover with remaining pie crust. If the pie crust is large enough, tuck the edges around the apples encasing the apples in pie crusts.
6. Brush top crust with egg wash and sprinkle with remaining 2 tbsp of sugar. Cut slits in top pie crust.
7. Place in oven and bake for 1 hour. An additional 10-15 minutes may be needed. Place a baking sheet under the pie to catch any drops that may occur. Towards the end of the cooking time, to stop any excessive browning, you may want to cover the edges or top with aluminum foil.
8. Once the pie is done, remove the pie from the oven and let it cool for at least 30 minutes, your patience will be rewarded!

15

Banana Upside Down Cake

Equipment:
Cast Iron Skillet

Ingredients:
For Cake:

- 1 ½ cups all purpose flour
- 1 ½ tsp baking powder
- ¾ tsp salt
- ½ cup vegetable oil
- ½ cup white sugar
- 2 tsp pure vanilla extract
- 1 large egg
- 1 large egg yolk
- 1 cup buttermilk, room temp.

For Bananas:

- ¼ cup unsalted butter

- ⅓ cup light brown sugar
- 4 large ripe bananas, sliced lengthwise
- ¼ tsp salt

Instructions:

1. Preheat the oven to 350°F.
2. In a skillet, melt butter over medium heat, add brown sugar and salt. Cook until dissolved, stirring continuously. Once dissolved, remove from heat and place bananas flat side down into the caramel. Cover all of the caramel.
3. In a medium bowl, whisk flour and baking powder. Set aside.
4. In a large bowl, whisk together oil, sugar and vanilla.
5. Add egg and yolk to the large bowl mixture and whisk until smooth. Add buttermilk and whisk again.
6. Add the dry ingredients to the wet, fold to combine. Do not over mix.
7. Pour the batter over the bananas and smooth out the top.
8. Place the skillet in the oven and bake for 35 - 40 minutes. Depending on your oven and for even cooking, you may want to rotate the pan halfway through cooking. Cook until a toothpick poked in the center comes out mostly clean.
9. When you remove the skillet from the oven, run a knife or spatula down the sides of the cake to help loosen while it cools. Let the cake sit for 5 minutes.
10. Place a plate or serving dish large enough to hold the cake on top of the skillet and carefully flip the cake onto the plate. Pick off any sticking pieces and place them back onto the cake. Let cool for about 20 minutes and ENJOY!

16

βαμ Barbecue Sauce

Equipment:
Cast Iron Skillet

Ingredients:

- 1 (24oz) container ketchup
- 1 cup water
- 2 ½ tbsp. worcestershire sauce
- 2 tbsp. apple cider vinegar
- 1 tbsp. cayenne pepper
- ½ tbsp smoked paprika
- 1 cup brown sugar
- 1 jalapeno pepper
- 1 serrano pepper
- ½ red bell pepper
- 1 garlic clove
- ⅓ onion
- 3 strips bacon
- liquid smoke or mesquite smoking chips

Instructions:

1. Fry bacon how you prefer your bacon done. Crumble/cut bacon into tiny pieces. If you cooked the bacon in your cast iron pan, wipe out extra fat and grease before moving on. You can leave a little to add flavor and help with lubrication of veggies.
2. Mince the onion, red bell pepper, jalapeno pepper, serrano pepper, and garlic, cook until caramelized and tender.
3. With everything in the cast iron pan add wet ingredients. (Water, ketchup, worcestershire sauce, and apple cider vinegar.) Bring to a simmer stirring often.
4. Once simmering, add dry ingredients.(Cayenne pepper, smoked paprika, brown sugar.)
5. Simmer mixture for approximately 30 minutes to thicken.
6. At this point you can add a small amount of liquid smoke to your sauce or smoke the sauce on the grill with the mesquite smoking chips to add a smokey flavor.

Some friends and I came up with this sauce while in college. We cooked everything in a cast iron skillet on a charcoal grill. We cooked everything in that pan and at the end, once the sauce was well combined and been simmering for a while, we moved the pan off of the coals so that it was still heated and added the smoking chips to the coal for about an additional 30 minutes. IT'S SO GOOD!

17

Conclusion

Throughout this book, I've touched on a lot of things. I know it's a lot to keep in mind, but, once you get past the initial learning and seasoning stages, it's really not too difficult. My goal was to give you something handy and helpful for you on your cast iron journey. If you're new to cast iron, hopefully this book was able to provide you some much needed information and processes for taking care of and preparing your cast iron. If you are already a cast iron owner and had a wealth of knowledge, this book was probably very basic to you, but I hope it was able to open your mind just a little bit. I am just like all of you in that I can be set in my ways too. Especially when it comes to the ritualistic care that comes with cast iron owners and users, we can be very stubborn. I've opened my mind while making this book, hopefully you were able to too.

I hope, if you've made it this far, that you have followed the pages of this book and now have a beautiful useful piece of cast iron cookware. Whether it's new, passed down from your family, or found in a garage sale. I hope that these words have helped you understand and show you how to care for your pans. With all of the information throughout the book if you have any questions, most of the issues you run into should be touched on or at least the solution to them should be in here somewhere.

If you find this book helpful, let myself or others know. The recipes within are fairly basic as well. They are in these pages to help you get comfortable and understand the versatility of the pan. I can't wait to hear from you about what you think about the book, or the food you create while using your pan. If you follow the words provided in this book and apply the proper care to your cookware, I have no doubt that these pieces can last for decades and be passed down from generation to generation.

Take care and happy cooking!

18

Resources

Gritzer, D. (2019, October 24). *How to season a cast iron pan (it's easier than you think!)*. Serious Eats. Retrieved September 10, 2022, from https://www.seriouseats.com/how-to-season-cast-iron-pans-skillets-cookware

Menghini, J. (2022, September 26). *Rustic skillet apple pie recipe*. Hostess At Heart. Retrieved October 1, 2022, from https://hostessatheart.com/skillet-apple-pie/

Neal. (2022, September 5). *The best oil for seasoning cast iron - and what not to use!* The Flat Top King. Retrieved October 1, 2022, from https://theflattopking.com/best-oil-for-seasoning-cast-iron/

Sheehan, J. (2021, March 19). *Caramelized banana upside-down cake recipe on food52*. Food52. Retrieved October 1, 2022, from https://food52.com/recipes/76561-caramelized-banana-upside-down-cake

Uno Casa. (2021, March 15). *Best oil for seasoning cast-iron: Pros & Cons of 9 oil options*. Uno Casa. Retrieved October 1, 2022, from https://uno

casa.com/blogs/tips/best-oil-for-seasoning-cast-iron

Welles, B. (2021, March 30). *Don's appliances: Pittsburgh, PA.* Don's Appliances. Retrieved October 1, 2022, from https://www.donsapplia nces.com/blog/what-is-induction-cooking-and-how-does-it-work

Wikimedia Foundation. (2022, October 1). *Cast-Iron Cookware.* Wikipedia. Retrieved October 1, 2022, from https://en.wikipedia.org/wiki/Cast-iron_cookware#:~:text=Types%20of%20cast%20iron%20cookware,woks%2C%20potjies%2C%20and%20karahi.

Xie, J. (2021, November 1). *How to season a cast iron pan so that it lasts forever.* Delish. Retrieved August 1, 2022, from https://www.delish.com/cooking/recipe-ideas/a32937364/how-to-season-a-cast-iron-pan/

www.ingramcontent.com/pod-product-compliance
Lightning Source LLC
Chambersburg PA
CBHW070759020526
44118CB00036B/2136